Puppy Training Guide for Kids

How to Train Your Dog or Puppy for Children, Following a Beginners Step-By-Step Guide: Includes Potty Training, 101 Dog Tricks, Socializing Skills, and More

By Lucy Williams

Table of Contents

Table of Contents

Table of Contents 2
Introduction 5
Welcome Home: The First Days Home 6

    Puppy Proofing 6
    Toys and Treats 7
    Rules and Bedtimes 9

Training Basics 11

    When to Start Training 11

        When to Potty Train 11
        When to Socialize 12
        When to Teach Tricks and Commands 12

    FUNdamentals of Training 13

        Positive Reinforcement 14
        Take it Slow and Stay Positive 15

    The First Commands 15

Let the Training Begin! 18

    Making Friends 18

        Socializing Starts at Home 18
        Baby Steps 19

    Using the Bathroom 22
    Simple Commands 25

        Sit 25
        Lie Down 27
        Stay 28

Circus Dog 31

Spin 31
Roll Over 32
Army Crawl 34

Hey,

Before we start, I want to tell you about an exclusive offer just for readers of this book...

When starting training your dog or puppy, the one thing that you must have is a training checklist to track your four legged best friend's progress. If don't implement this you are setting yourself up for failure before you have even started.

Creating a checklist yourself is super inconvenient, right?

Well yes, it would be, but luckily for you, I have partnered up with Bark Insights. Who are giving away their highly rated dog & puppy training checklist to help you track your pooches' progress seamlessly!

Best thing about this exclusive offer is it 100% FREE, no-strings-attached. Bark Insights usually charge $49 for this exact same checklist to their customers

All you need to do to claim your FREE the training checklist; is type in on your search browsers URL – free.barkinsights.com

Once you are on the web page, fill out the required information that Bark Insights asks for; this should only take less than 1 minute of your time. Then straight away in your email inbox you will receive the checklist that has helped 10,000's of people around the world train their dogs more effectively.

Before reading any further, please do this NOW as I may refer back to the checklist throughout this book!

free.barkinsights.com

Introduction

Training your best friend to behave and do tricks is one of the best things you can do for them and for you. If your parents have just gotten you a new puppy or dog, then the chances are they aren't listening to you at all. If you don't teach them to listen to you then they never will. It might be funny at first when the dog jumps up on you or chews one of your shoes, but it won't stay funny for very long.

Training a puppy or dog isn't easy, but that doesn't mean it can't be fun. You can make training lots of fun for both you and your new best friend. The important thing is to work together and make sure you get all the help you need from your parents. Trust me, your puppy or dog will love it.

You don't have to feel bad for them when you train them. Your best friend will love it just as much as you do, and it will make them a lot happier in the long run. A dog or puppy enjoys spending time with their human and making their human happy. While you're training them, they will be spending a lot of time with you and making you happy, so you're giving them everything they want.

A well trained dog makes for a better and healthier relationship. Your best friend will learn to listen and communicate with you. You will learn what they want and what makes them happy. This will make it easier for the two of you to make each other happy and enjoy the time you spend together.

It's a good thing you found this book, because it will teach you everything you need to know to fully train your new best friend the easiest and most fun way. In this book you'll find social training, potty training, house training, simple commands, and some pretty cool dog tricks too. You'll find everything you need to help train your new best friend and have fun doing it.

Let's get started!

Welcome Home: The First Days Home

First impressions are important, and you want to make sure that your new best friend's first day home is the best. You're probably excited and jumping up and down with joy. You can't wait to meet your new friend and spend as much time with him or her as possible, but I bet you're also scared. It's okay to be scared at first. You're about to bring a new puppy home, and you're not sure if you know what to do. You can look to your parents for guidance, but you can also look to this book.

Being excited to meet your new best friend and being scared at the same time is perfectly normal. As long as you know you're prepared for their first day home then you don't have to worry about anything. Their first few days home are the most important. Let's make sure you make the best first impression and welcome them home the right way.

Puppy Proofing

The first thing you need to do before you or your parents bring your new puppy home is make the house a safe place for them. Puppy proofing is a lot like baby proofing. You can ask your parents what they had to do to make the house a safe place for you when you were a baby. Then ask them to help you do the same thing for the puppy.

A puppy won't be able to tell what is safe and what is dangerous. You know how to use a set of stairs and you won't jump into the pool if you don't know how to swim. However, if you have stairs or a pool, your new puppy will not know how to properly act around them and they may hurt themselves. This is the important part of puppy proofing your house. Find all the places and objects in the house that may become harmful or dangerous to your new best friend and remove or block them off. Make sure you ask your parents to help you with this step.

It's important you do this before you bring your new puppy to the house. That way it's easier to just put them down and let them explore their new home with you. Puppy proofing is an important step to welcoming them home.

Toys and Treats

There are a few things you should have before your puppy comes home for the first time. Ask your parents to get all of these things and make sure that they do. You don't want to bring your new best friend home, realize you don't have something you need, and then run off looking for it or wait until the next day. It's better you have all of these things there and ready for when they first come home.

Here's a simple list of the things you should have before you bring your puppy home:

1. Dog Food

This one is a must considering how hungry your puppy is going to be. If you have a puppy, you will need a specific puppy food. Your puppy will need different nutrients than a fully grown dog, so they can't just eat any dog food. High quality food is the best for them and will help them grow strong and happy.

2. Water and Food Bowls

Your puppy is going to be thirsty from day one, and you can't expect them to eat that food off of the floor. The best bowls to get for your pet are stainless steel bowls. These bowls are easy to clean and will be healthier for your puppy in the long run. Make sure your parents get the right sized bowls as well. A puppy won't need something big, but when they grow you may need to replace the small bowls with something bigger.

Fill the water and food bowls and put them in an easy to reach place for you puppy's arrival.

3. Dog Bed

If you sleep in a comfortable bed at night then why can't your puppy do the same? Before you bring your puppy home, ask your parents to get them a nice dog bed to sleep on. Don't buy something small just because your puppy is small. If you expect your puppy is going to grow into a big dog then it may be a good idea to get something bigger to begin with. Your puppy won't mind what size it is, and, as they grow bigger, your parents won't have to replace the dog bed all the time.

Set up the dog bed in a safe area for your puppy somewhere near the water and food bowls.

4. Walking Equipment

You'll probably want to take your new puppy for a walk straight away. Save the walk for the next day and keep the first day calm and fun inside the house. It's still a good idea to get everything you need for a walk before you bring your puppy home, just in case.

You'll need a dog collar or harness and leash. Remember that your puppy is still growing, and you need a collar or harness that adjusts. That way if they grow bigger you can still use the same collar or harness. You will also need some poop bags and a poop bag holder. Yes, you will have to clean up your new friend's poop when you're out on a walk, because it is the nice thing to do. If you don't then some poor person might walk into it and that would ruin their day.

5. Treats and Toys

You love eating things like chocolate and ice-cream and playing with your favorite games and toys right? Well your new puppy is going to love doing the same thing. Ask your parents to get them a bag of dog treats and some toys to play with for their first day home. You don't need to go overboard with this. Your new puppy is still learning what they love to eat and how they like to play. They may not enjoy all the toys you get them, so it's a good idea to buy only a few for their first day and learn what they like as you go along.

Get one soft toy, like a teddy bear, a squeaky toy that makes a noise (make sure it's not too loud for your puppy's sensitive ears; a bell that rings may be a better choice), and a chew toy. These three are the perfect first toys for a new puppy. Their first treats should be small, easy to chew, and easy to swallow.

6. Dog Tags and Microchip

You don't want to risk losing your best friend if they get out of the house or get loose while out on a walk. Ask your parents to get a dog tag, with their name and a way to contact your parents on it, and a collar to put it on. Make sure your puppy wears this collar all the time. Also ask your parents to get your new puppy a microchip. This is something they put underneath your dog's skin. It doesn't hurt them, and if they ever get lost someone will be able to scan the chip, see who the owners are, and return your puppy home.

Make sure your parents get this for your puppy straight away.

That's all the things you need to get for your puppy's first day home. Here are a few things you might need to get later on:

1. Dog Brush

If you have a hairy dog, then you need a brush. Try using the brush once a day if they have a lot of hair. This will make sure they don't get a lot of knots or get really dirty. Brushing is something your puppy is going to love!

2. Dog Toothpaste and a Toothbrush

You need to brush your teeth, and so does your new best friend. The only problem is they don't know how to brush their own teeth. You'll have to help them brush their teeth regularly.

3. Dog Shampoo and Towel

You probably wash your hair whenever you bathe, but you can't use your shampoo on your puppy. You need dog shampoo to use on them. It has special ingredients to keep their fur healthy and clean. Just like your dog can't brush his own teeth, he can't wash his own fur. You can help him by bathing him at least once every two weeks, unless he gets dirty easily. If he rolls in mud or dirt, then you'll have to wash him sooner than that.

Rules and Bedtimes

When you were growing up you had a lot of rules that you had to follow or else your parents would have been upset with you. Your new puppy has to follow some rules as well. You can think of them as either your new best friend or your new little brother or sister. They need to follow some rules just like you had to.

You and your parents need to figure out what the rules are before you bring your new puppy home. You need to list the rules and stick to them from the beginning. You can't allow your new puppy to sleep on your bed from day one, then decide later on that they aren't' allowed to do that anymore. This will confuse them. If you want them on the bed or not, you have to decide that from day one and keep up with it.

Training usually starts on the first day, and most people don't realize that. A puppy will show behavior on their very first day home, and you and your parents need to decide if you like or want that behavior later on. If a puppy jumps up on you their first few days home and you allow it, they will see that as normal. When the puppy gets bigger, they will still jump up on you like they did when they were a puppy. This may be more dangerous and sore, especially if they start doing it to other people out on the street. You can't punish them for this because you've been letting them do it since they were a puppy, so they don't understand that it is wrong. To avoid many other problems like this, set up the rules from the start.

Remember, whatever behavior your puppy learns from the first few days will stick with them for the rest of their lives. This is the start of their training. The rules you and your parents come up with the very first day your puppy is in his new home are going to be the guidelines for them to follow. The rules will help them know what is wrong and what is right. This is the most important first step you need to take for your puppies training and it starts on day one.

Training Basics

There are a few things you need to know about training your dog before you can start the training process. You need to start with the basics. Things like when to start training your dog, how to start training your dog, and the most important things you can teach them. You need to understand all of these before you can move forward.

When to Start Training

Training your dog to have good habits and be obedient can start as early as possible, but there are some things that you just can't teach your dog until they reach a certain age. It's true that forming good habits for your puppy should start the very first day you bring them home. You can start teaching your puppy things like not jumping up on the couch or not chewing the furniture as soon as you get them home. However, things like potty training and social training can only be started when your puppy reaches a certain age.

When to Potty Train

It's likely when you bring your puppy home for the first time they won't be house trained. This means that you can expect them to have a few accidents. You can start potty training your dog as soon as you bring them home, but it may be difficult if they are younger than 12 to 16 weeks. Until the puppy reaches this age, they have little to no control over their bladder. This means that they can't control when they go to the bathroom, and they can't hold it in until someone opens the door for them.

Until your puppy reaches 12 to 16 weeks of age, you will find it very difficult to potty train them. This doesn't mean that you can't try. You can limit accidents in the house and make the training easier for when they are old enough if you start the training early.

If you do start the potty training early just remember that even if your puppy understands what you're trying to teach them, you may not see results until they are old enough.

When to Socialize

Socializing a puppy is completely different to potty training and so the start time for this is also different. A puppy usually starts socialization as soon as it opens its eyes and starts moving around. The first bit of socialization a puppy gets is with its siblings and mother. This helps socialize the dog to other puppies, but this isn't enough. The puppy also needs to be socialized with a wide variety of people, animals, and objects.

Socializing your puppy can take place as early as 7 weeks old. Once your puppy reaches this age, they will be very open to meeting and getting to know new people, new animals, and new things. Once they are older than 14 to 16 weeks, they become more closed off to the idea of meeting something new. The best time to socialize your dog is between 7 to 14 or 16 weeks of age.

When to Teach Tricks and Commands

Puppies have very short attention spans at any age, but they are always eager to learn and to please their owner. You'll be surprised to know that you can start teaching your puppy tricks, like sit and stay, as early as 7 weeks old. The best way to train a dog as young as 7 weeks is with a reward system, which I will be discussing further on in the book.

Some believe that the formal training, like commands and tricks, should be delayed until your dog is at least 6 months old. This is a bad idea. When your dog reaches this age, they are already past the eager learner stage and are transitioning into becoming an adult dog. Some of the things they learned as a puppy have already been hardwired into them at this age. If you only start training your dog at 6 months, you will find that they learned a lot of things when they were younger that they now have to unlearn and relearn the right way. It's far better not to wait till this period to start training. Formal training can start as early as around 7 weeks of age and should be kept up until your dog is a fully grown adult.

Just keep in mind that your puppy's attention span is extremely short at this point, and you will only be able to teach them for about 15 minutes a time, at the most. You can teach them multiple times throughout the day even for a short time. They will be happy that you started training them that young and they will enjoy it, especially if you use the reward system.

When training your puppy to do anything, whether it is potty training, socialization, or learning to do tricks, you can start as soon as possible. Just remember that it will be difficult at first for the puppy to remember the things you are trying to teach them and actually put it into practice. Potty training will be the most difficult until they reach the proper age, but it will be worth it and make the whole process easier in the long run.

FUNdamentals of Training

Training can be fun, as long as you keep in mind all of the important information that comes with the training process. There are a few fundamentals you have to keep in mind for both yours and your puppy's sake. These fundamentals will make both your lives easier.

Positive Reinforcement

Positive reinforcement is part of the reward system I was talking about earlier. A puppy learns best when it is rewarded for good behavior, however, a puppy learns badly when it is punished for bad behavior. You should never punish your puppy by yelling at them or hitting them for doing something you don't want them to do. This could make the bad behavior worse and even reinforce it.

To understand how this works, you need to understand that a puppy sees attention from you as a reward. They will see any attention from you as a reward for what they are doing. Even if you are yelling at them for barking or jumping up on you, they see this as receiving attention from you and for them this is a reward. Therefore, it makes sense that to punish them for doing something bad you should simply ignore them. If your puppy is doing something that you don't want them to do, like barking or jumping up, then you shouldn't yell at them; instead, you should ignore them until they stop doing it. When they stop doing it then you should reward them by petting them, praising them, or giving them a treat. Soon your puppy will learn that they don't get attention from you if they bark or jump up, but they do get attention from you when they aren't doing it. Eventually they will learn and stop doing it.

This is the power of positive reinforcement. You encourage your puppy to do something you want them to do, like sit nicely for a treat or not bark at people at the door, by rewarding them with treats and attention. You discourage your puppy from doing something you don't want them to do not by hitting or yelling at them, but by ignoring them. This is the best and most powerful form of training. Your puppy receives a reward for good and wanted behavior and is ignored for doing bad or unwanted behavior. A puppy learns best using this method.

Take it Slow and Stay Positive

I mentioned before how your puppy will have a short attention span, and they will only be able to learn for a short amount of time. It's important that you remember this. The things you want to teach your dog will have to be broken up into small parts, and you need to teach each part to them slowly. What your puppy needs from you is patience and to listen. They will let you know when they have had enough training. It's up to you to listen to them and stop the training session when they are done for the day. If you push them too far too soon, they will have a bad experience with training and not want to do it again.

Move slowly for your puppy and only teach them for 10 to 15 minutes at a time. Always reward them at the end of the session so they have a good experience that makes them want to do it again when they're ready. Be prepared for your puppy to get confused and have to start from the beginning again. If your puppy fails at a trick, it isn't their fault and you shouldn't be angry with them or punish them. Stay positive and try again. Your puppy will be able to read your actions and if they think you are upset with them, they won't learn anything you're trying to teach them.

Training for your puppy should be happy, rewarding, and positive. Move at your puppy's pace, not yours. That's all you need to know to successfully train your puppy.

The First Commands

There are a lot of tricks you will want to teach your puppy, but you should start with the first commands. These commands make up the base movements for other tricks and they help your dog learn to be obedient and have good manners. These commands are also good for safety reasons when taking your dog out into public, and they work great if taught properly.

1. Sit

This is the very first command you should teach your puppy. It forms the base for all other commands and is very useful in lots of situations. Once your puppy knows to sit when told, everything else will be made easier.

2. Lay Down

Your puppy will need to know the sit command to learn this one, and it is a very useful trick. It should be the second command your puppy learns.

3. Stay

This is the third command you should teach your puppy, and they can't learn it properly until they know how to sit. This is very useful for keeping your dog safe and teaching them other commands and manners.

These commands are the building blocks for your puppy to learn good behavior, build good habits, and learn a lot of fun tricks in the future.

Hey,

As mentioned at the start of this book, you have an exclusive offer available to you for a short period of time.

In case you forgot to claim your 100% FREE, no strings attached dog & puppy training checklist by Bark Insights.

Please can you make sure to do so NOW!

The reason for this is in the next coming chapters I will be discussing and referring back to parts of the checklist that Bark Insights has created for you to improve your dog training experience.

It will be pivotal to have this checklist available at all times as when training your dog or puppy, the training checklist will help you to look back on how far your four legged best friend has come.

In case you forgot how to claim your FREE copy of the checklist, is type in on your search browser URL – free.barkinsights.com

Remember, before reading any further, please do this NOW as I will refer back to parts of the checklist throughout this book!

free.barkinsights.com

Let the Training Begin!

You are now ready to begin training your puppy how to be a good dog. You know everything you need to know; now you just need to know what to do. Ahead you will find everything you need to know about how to potty train, socialize, and fully train your new best friend. Have fun!

Making Friends

Socializing your puppy involves a lot more than just making friends with other dogs, animals, and humans. Socializing a puppy properly is a very delicate thing to do and it is very important. The socializing your puppy receives at a young age will determine how they act and what their personality is when they are a full grown dog. Socializing involves introducing your puppy to new sights, sounds, objects, animals, people, situations, and places in a positive way so they learn to see those things and react to them with a positive attitude.

Socializing your puppy begins as soon as possible and should be handled carefully. You might want to ask your parents to help you with this. Follow these steps and you'll be fine.

Socializing Starts at Home

Socializing a puppy usually starts at home with you and your family. You can give your puppy positive experiences that they can then associate with later experiences in life. From the very first day you bring your new best friend home, you can start socializing them.

You can start with the easy stuff. You can start by getting them used to being held, touched, and pet in different places. Dogs usually don't like it when you touch their tail or paws, so avoid these areas at first. Another thing you can do is have some active play time with your puppy. Playtime is a great way for a puppy to learn how to play with others and how to play properly with dogs even.

When it comes to socializing your puppy at home, there are two major things you need to teach them:

1. To not be afraid of hands or being touched by people
2. To not bite or be aggressive during play time

These are the most important and easiest things you can teach a dog during socialization during their first few days at home.

Baby Steps

When your puppy is about 7 weeks old they can start being introduced to other people and other animals. You'll want to start small and take baby steps with this one. If your puppy gets over excited or scared, it could ruin the session and give them a bad experience that will haunt them for further sessions.

Here are some of the first baby steps for you to take:

1. Introduce your puppy to some friends

Either bring your own friends over or ask your parents to bring some of their friends or the neighbors over. Whoever you invite over to meet your puppy needs to follow a set of rules. They need to be calm and positive towards the puppy. They need to greet them gently and follow the puppy's actions. If the puppy seems scared then they have to back off and wait for the puppy to come to them. You don't want to force your puppy into a situation that makes them feel uncomfortable or it will ruin the experience.

They need to pet your puppy and play with them gently. Have only one friend over at a time and have a different friend come over each day. This will get your puppy used to seeing different people and playing with them. This is how you socialize a puppy with other humans.

Later on you can bring more and more people over to make sure your puppy is comfortable with a group of people around them. Do this slowly. Have two to three people over and then slowly increase the number. Remember to take baby steps, be calm and gentle, and follow your puppy's actions. They will tell you if they are uncomfortable or scared.

2. Introduce your puppy to another dog

When introducing your puppy to another dog, it's best to start on neutral ground with a calm, already socialized dog. Neutral ground means a place that doesn't belong to your puppy or the other dog. Even at a young age your puppy will have already claimed your house as their territory and bringing another dog into their territory can be a bad start to socialization.

The dog park or just a piece of the street can be a good start. You need a place that isn't entirely free of distractions but isn't too busy. You want your puppy to be focused on meeting the new dog but you don't want that dog to be the only thing for your puppy to focus on. Too much distraction can overwhelm your puppy and too little distraction can intimidate them.

When introducing your puppy to another dog have them on a leash to begin with. Don't let the dogs face each other off. Looking another dog in the eye for too long is an act of aggression and could start a fight. Avoid eye contact and let them instead sniff each other.

It's better that the other dog is calm, or maybe even old and not too big, so they won't be too excited or want to play with your puppy at first. This way your puppy can take their time. For the first play date you can take your puppy and the other dog for a walk together. Then your puppy has other things to put their mind on, and they get used to having another dog around.

You can increase the socialization by introducing your puppy to more dogs, but only one at a time at first. Have them play together at some stage and then introduce more dogs at once. Move slowly with these steps and listen to your puppy. If they are scared or uncomfortable, pull them out of the situation and slow it down.

After your dog is comfortable with other dogs, you can take them to a busy dog park. Keep their leash on at first to see how they handle it. If they are too excited or too scared, you shouldn't take the leash off. Stay on the outside of the park at first and allow your puppy some time to look at the dogs and watch them from a distance. If they seem calm and interested then you can take them into the dog park and slowly introduce them to the other dogs.

3. Introduce your puppy to other animals

Next you want to introduce your puppy to other pets and animals. The more animals you can introduce them to the better. You can start with cats. Make sure you introduce them to a cat that is calm and already used to having dogs around. Cats are the easiest to start with. Next you can try birds and other animals.

You may want to consider a trip to a petting zoo or a farm nearby if they allow dogs. You can keep your puppy on a leash and introduce them to many other animals, big and small, and they will slowly get used to them. Remember to move slowly with this. Your puppy should be more open to meeting new animals after they have met other dogs. They will be curious and cautious at first and that is good. Don't push them and move at their pace. If you do that you should be fine.

4. Introduce your puppy to various objects, places, and situations

There are several things you need to introduce your puppy to as soon as possible so that they are not scared of them later on in life. These are simple objects, places, or experiences. You should move slowly and listen to your puppy while introducing them to these various things. Here is a short list of introductions you should make:

- Cars (moving and standing still)
- Riding in a car (start short, then make it longer with lots of breaks, and then finally a long, non-stop car ride)
- Bicycles and Motorbikes (moving and standing still)
- Busy malls or streets
- Busy roads with lots of cars

- Different grounds (grass, tar, sand, rock, tiles, carpet, wood floors, etc.)
- Wheelchairs or crutches and canes
- Different people (wearing sunglasses, wearing a hood, using an umbrella, with a beard, etc.)
- Big signs and small road signs

These are only a few things you can introduce your puppy to early on so they aren't scared of it later in life. Do this slowly and, as always, don't force your puppy to do something they don't want to do. If your puppy is interested or curious then move forward. If they aren't then slow down and remove them from the situation.

Using the Bathroom

House training your puppy will take a long time. It will take longer than teaching them a couple of commands or socializing them. It's believed that it could take 4 to 6 months to fully potty train a dog. However, those numbers are dependent on the dog's environment and how often and hard you enforce the training. If a puppy moves from one house to another house in the middle of their potty training then you may need to start all over. The good thing is they will learn it faster the second time. Potty training the right way requires patience and a lot of commitment as you will be doing this with them every day.

Here are the steps you can take to start potty training your puppy:

Step 1: You should start by keeping your puppy in a small area of the house where you can watch them or keep your eye on them. Doing this ensures that your puppy is not allowed to wander around the house alone and go to the bathroom whenever they want. It will minimize any accidents. Here are some options for confining your puppy:

1. A small room such as the bathroom
2. In a crate, this is useful if you are doing crate training
3. In a puppy pen made out of baby gates

You can cover the floors in newspaper or just leave them as is if the floor is made of tiles. Keep the puppy's water and bed in the same place so they have easy access to it.

Step 2: Once you have confined your puppy to a small space, you can begin the training. The first thing you should do is come up with a feeding schedule. You should feed your puppy at least three times a day at the same time every day. Your puppy needs to eat during the feeding times and their food must be taken away after they are done eating. Feeding your puppy this way means you will know exactly when they need to go to the bathroom.

You should take your puppy outside after each meal and wait for them to use the bathroom. When they do use the bathroom you should praise them and act very excited. This will send your puppy signals letting them know that what they have done is very good.

Step 3: There are other times you should take your puppy out to the bathroom to make sure they understand what you want from them.

Your puppy should be taken out first thing in the morning to use the bathroom. You can expect your puppy to have had an accident in the middle of the night for the first few weeks. This is because your puppy's bladder is still weak. They will still need to be taken out to use the bathroom in the morning and last thing at night before going to bed.

You also need to take your puppy out during the day every 30 minutes to an hour. As the puppy gets older you will not need to do this as often. You will also need to take the puppy out after they wake up from a nap

You should write down a list of all the times you need to take your puppy out to use the bathroom, just so you can keep track of it. Here is a list for you to copy from:

1. Take your puppy out first thing in the morning.
2. Take your puppy out after all three meals during the day.
3. Take your puppy out every 30 minutes or hour during the day.
4. Take your puppy out just before going to bed.

Step 4: Always take your puppy to the same spot every time you take them out. Their scent will still be there from the last time they went. The scent will encourage your puppy to go to the bathroom in or near that spot again. You will have to stay with your puppy while they are outside until they are potty trained, so you can make sure they are actually using the bathroom.

Every single time your puppy uses the bathroom outside you must praise them and reward them for it. They will eventually associate the action of using the bathroom outside with the reward and the positive attention.

The last thing you will have to do is clean whatever accidents your puppy has inside the house properly. You need to clean it in a way where it doesn't keep the scent. Your puppy will be able to smell the scent, and it will encourage them to go in that spot again. You want to discourage going inside as much as possible.

If your puppy does have an accident, you can't punish or yell at them for it. By the time you find the accident, it's probably too late to punish them. They won't understand why you're punishing them even if you show them their accident. Another reason you can't punish them is because they will associate bad feelings with the act of using the bathroom. This can ruin the training completely. If you do catch your puppy in the middle of their accident then you can try and stop them by lifting them up and taking them outside quickly. This is the best way to stop accidents from happening and also make sure your puppy understands what kind of behavior you want from them.

You must continue to follow these steps throughout your puppy's young life. In a few months your puppy will be better at holding it in overnight and you will see little to no accidents. You won't have to take them out as often and you can start allowing them to roam through the rest of the house. At this point you can start waiting for your puppy to go to the door by themselves. This is the first step to them telling you that they want to go outside to use the bathroom instead of taking them out on a schedule. When they start doing this, you don't have to stay outside with them. You should always praise and reward them for wanting to go outside.

You must keep this training up until your puppy is at least 6 months old, but the older they get the less you will have to do. The first three months are the hardest for potty training but the results will be worth the work. Your puppy will feel happier and more dependent when they get to control when they go out.

Simple Commands

If you teach your puppy these simple commands, both your lives, and further training, will be made much easier. All of these training tips involve using positive reinforcement, the reward system, and something called the luring technique. The luring technique involves using a treat or reward of some kind to lure your puppy into the position of the trick and then giving the treat or reward to them when they are in that position.

If you follow the steps, you can teach each command to your puppy within a week if they are at least 7 weeks old.

Sit

This is the very first command any puppy should learn, and it will make teaching them every other command and trick easier. This trick is also the easiest trick for your puppy to learn using the reward system and the luring technique.

Here's what you need to start:

1. A handful of small treats that your puppy can eat easily and quickly

2. A quiet area with no distractions

3. A leash may be necessary

Here's what you do:

Step 1: Have your puppy standing in front of you in a quiet room with a comfortable blanket or carpet on the floor. This makes the whole situation a lot more comfortable for the puppy. There has to be no distractions or it could ruin the session. Use a small treat to hold your puppy's attention.

Step 2: Bring the treat low until it is directly in front of the puppy's face. Your puppy will attempt to grab the treat from your hand. This is normal and what you want to happen. When your puppy goes for the treat, slowly lift the treat up, above their head, and then slowly toward them. The puppy will follow the treat with their head. As their head lifts to follow the treat their butt will sit down on the ground. This is the sitting action you want from them.

The moment they are in the sitting position you can give them the treat and praise them. You need to repeat this step a couple of times until you are sure your puppy understands the movement and does it effortlessly without jumping for the treat or hesitating.

Step 3: At this point you can add the command word to the action. Right now your puppy has been associating the action of sitting with the action of you lifting the treat above their head. You want them to associate the command with the word for the command. Repeat step 2 but this time when your puppy enters the sitting position say loudly in a positive, happy voice, 'Sit!' If you do this every time, your puppy will start to associate the command with the word and not the action.

Repeat this step a couple of times before moving on.

Step 4: Now you need to move away from the luring technique and have your puppy sit using only the voice command. Have the treat in your hand so your puppy can see their reward for doing a good job. Don't move the treat above their head. Simply say in the same loud, positive, and happy voice "Sit!" Your puppy should already associate the word with the action of sitting and the reward at the end. Your puppy should sit when you tell them to, and if they do you must give them the reward and praise them.

The final step involves eliminating the presence of the treat entirely. You want your puppy to get used to the action and the word and then get them to do it even though they don't see a treat in sight. You can do this by replacing the treat with other rewards, such as praise, pets, and playtime. Your puppy needs to associate doing the right thing with a reward, but the reward doesn't have to be something they can eat.

The leash comes in when you want your puppy to follow the sit command even when you're out on a walk. At the moment, you've been doing the trick in a quiet, distraction-free area. When you go for a walk there will be a lot of things to distract your puppy and they won't listen to you when you tell them to sit. If you use the leash during your training sessions inside the house, they will learn to associate the leash with the command and that will make it easier to teach it to them while on a walk.

Lie Down

The lie down position is very useful if you don't want your puppy to get in the way or you want them to calm down for a moment. It's also a building block for some really cool tricks you can teach them later on. You will also be using the lure technique for this trick.

Here's what you need to start:

1. A handful of small treats that your puppy can eat quickly and easily

2. A quiet area with no distractions

Here's what you have to do:

Step 1: Start in a small area with little to no distractions. It should be only you and your puppy in the room. Place a blanket or carpet on the floor so your puppy is comfortable. To start, use a treat to grab your puppy's attention. Tell your puppy to sit. Once they are in the sit position place the treat in front of their face, but don't put it too close so they can grab it.

When you have your puppy's attention with the treat start moving it down towards the floor. Move it slowly. Move it all the way to the floor, then away from your puppy and towards your shoes. The puppy's head will follow the treat down until their body is lying on the floor. As soon as they enter the lie down position you should give them the treat, praise, and pet them.

Repeat this step a few times until your puppy gets into the lie down position quickly and easily.

Step 2: Now you can add the command to the action. Repeat step 1 but this time when your puppy enters the lie down position you should say the command loudly in a happy, positive voice. Say 'lie down!' or just 'down!'—it depends on which one you want. Repeat this over and over again so your puppy starts to associate the word with the action rather than the lure or the treat.

Repeat this step a couple of times.

Step 3: Now you want to eliminate the treat and lure all together. Have the treat visible at first but don't use the lure technique. Say the command. If your puppy lies down when you say it then give them their reward. Repeat this step to make sure they know the word equals the action. Eventually you want to have your puppy perform the trick with or without being able to see a treat. You can reward them if they do it, but you want them to do it even if they aren't expecting a reward of some kind.

Stay

The stay command is very useful inside or outside the house. This should be the third command you teach your puppy. It will take more than a week for your puppy to fully understand the command and stay even though you've left the room or walked a really far way away from them. You can't use the luring technique for this trick but you can use what your puppy knows from the sit and lie down commands.

Here's what you need to start:

1. A handful of small treats your puppy can eat quickly and easily
2. A quiet area with no distractions
3. A leash

Here's what you need to do:

Step 1: To start, you need to be alone with your puppy in a quiet, distraction free room. You can put a blanket or carpet on the floor so your puppy is comfortable. To start the trick you can have your puppy in the sit position or the lie down position. Both of the starting positions work and you can even test the stay command when your puppy is in both positions.

With your puppy in the sit or down position, you start in front of them with a treat in your hand. The treat will get their attention. Say 'stay!' loudly in a happy, positive voice and take a step backwards. Wait a moment, then repeat the command and take another step backwards. Repeat this action for about five steps then wait for a few seconds. Make sure to keep your eyes on them during the process. If your puppy doesn't move at all you can walk towards them and give them their reward. Remember to praise them as well as give them the treat.

Repeat this a couple times and slowly increase the amount of steps you take backwards and the amount of time you wait before giving them their reward. The main goal is that your puppy doesn't move from their spot to follow the treat.

Step 2: Once you've repeated step 1 a few times and your puppy hasn't moved to follow you or go for the treat then it's safe to move on. Now you want to increase the speed at which you move away from them. Show them the treat in your hand, tell them to stay, and walk backwards quickly until you are on the other end of the room. Make sure to maintain eye contact with your puppy. If they don't move, then stay at the other end of the room for a few seconds. Continue to show them the treat and keep eye contact while you count down the seconds. Then you can reward them.

Repeat this a few times, increasing the amount of time you wait at the other end of the room before giving your puppy their reward.

Increase the time until you are waiting for at least a minute. You can increase it more but that won't be necessary at this step.

If your puppy looks like they are about to move, simply repeat the command for them. Before you move on make sure they stay in one spot for the full minute without you having to repeat the command.

Step 3: The next step involves you moving to a bigger room and repeating step 2. You want to move further and further away from your puppy and wait longer before rewarding them. You need to make sure they are willing to wait for a long time, no matter how far away you get. The final step will involve you leaving your puppy in a room and asking them to stay until you get back. The testing point will be when your puppy can't see you or the reward but they still stay because they are told to.

When your puppy is able to stay still in a room, even after you've left the room for at least a minute, you can start removing the visible reward. Now you want to test that your puppy will perform the command even if they can't see a reward in your hand. They are doing it because they want to.

Later on you can add a leash to the trick and start from step 1. This is for when you're walking your puppy. Dropping the leash and telling them to stay will help if you drop or lose the leash while out on a walk. Before your puppy can get away from you, you can tell them to stay. That will give you time to pick the leash back up again before they run away. Test this move slowly, starting indoors and going through the steps, then move outdoors in an enclosed space. Test it properly before moving into an open space outside.

Circus Dog

Everybody loves it when a dog can perform a really fun, cool trick. You can easily teach your puppy to do cool things so you can show off to your friends. Make sure your puppy has already learned the above commands before teaching them any of these tricks. They are simple and really fun. You and your dog will love learning them together.

Spin

Teaching your puppy to spin on command is really cool and impressive. It's also really simple. All you have to do is use the lure technique and repeat it over and over again until your puppy gets it.

Here's what you need to start:

1. A handful of small treats your puppy can eat easily and quickly
2. A quiet, distraction free room
3. The sit command

Here's what to do:

Step 1: Start in a small room with just you and your puppy and put a blanket or carpet on the floor. It's easier if your puppy knows how to sit, because this is how they will start the trick. Your puppy will feel more confident if they start with something they know.

With your puppy in the sitting position, take a treat in your hand and show it to them. Hold it in front of their face and when they move for it pull the treat away. You want to pull the treat around in a circle while keeping it in front of your puppy's face. They will get up and follow the treat. If you use the lure correctly, your puppy will follow the treat and spin in place. If they do this, tell them to sit at the end of it and then give them the treat. Remember to praise and pet them. Make a big deal out of it so your puppy feels excited about doing it again.

Repeat this step a few times.

Step 2: Now you want to add the verbal command to the trick. This is really easy to do. Repeat step 1 again but this time, just before using the lure to get your puppy to spin in place, say your verbal command. The verbal command can be anything you want it to be. You can say 'spin!' which is a simple one or you can say something like 'circus dog!' It doesn't matter what you choose as long as you teach your puppy to associate the word with the action.

Repeat this step multiple times before moving on.

Step 3: Your puppy should be used to the action and the word associated with it before you move on to this step. Now you want to remove the lure. Hold the treat so your puppy can see it and tell them to spin. If they don't do it straight away mimic the luring action above their head but not too close to them. Your puppy has associated the luring movement with the trick so they may need to see that again. Mimic the action in the air quickly while saying the command again. If they do it then reward them. If they don't then you need to go back to step 2.

The goal is to remove the visible treat and the lure action all together. Eventually you want your dog to spin when you ask them to, no matter what. If you want your puppy to spin in both directions, you will have to teach each direction one at a time. For this you may need to keep the lure movement in the air so your puppy doesn't get confused with which way you want them to turn.

Roll Over

This is a really cute and simple trick you can teach your puppy. If your puppy learns this trick you can teach them how to play dead and other similar tricks as well. You have to start with this one first. Your puppy needs to know how to lie down before they can learn this trick.

Here's what you need to start:

1. A handful of small treats that your puppy can quickly and easily eat
2. A quiet, distraction free room
3. The lie down command

Here's how you do it:

Step 1: Start in a distraction free room with just you and your puppy. Put a blanket or carpet on the floor. Your puppy needs to know the lie down position in order to perform this trick as it is a part of it.

Have the treat in your hand and ask your puppy to lie down. When they do, get down on your knees and hold the treat in front of their face. Move the treat slightly to the side, then up a little, and over your puppy's head all the way to the other side. Move the treat slowly so your puppy can follow it.

If you do this right your puppy will follow the treat with their head, causing them to turn over onto their back and roll onto their other side. Keep moving the treat until they are back in the lie down position and then you can reward them.

Repeat this step a couple of times until the movement is easy for your puppy. If they struggle to roll over all the way you can help them by nudging their side a bit.

Step 2: When the movement is easy for your puppy to perform, you can add the verbal command to the trick. Repeat step 1 but this time before using the lure you can say your command. Again, this can be anything you want it to be. For now we will use the words "roll over."

Repeat step 1 with the verbal command a couple of times. This is a harder trick than the ones before it. Therefore you will have to repeat this more times to make sure your puppy gets it. You will know they understand the trick if they can roll over easily each time you do it. If they struggle and need help, you need to keep going.

Step 3: You can move on to step three, which is eliminating the lure technique and using only the verbal command to get your puppy to perform the trick. You will still need to show your puppy the treat to start with so they know what they are doing the trick for. Again, you may also need to use the action of the lure to make sure your puppy understands what you want from them.

Puppies are smarter than you think and they will understand the trick eventually. Some puppies may require more time and practice before they get the trick right. You have to keep at it and practice as much as possible.

Army Crawl

This trick is really cool and cute. You and your puppy are going to love learning this trick together. Your puppy will need to know the lie down command to be able to learn this trick.

Here's what you need to do:

1. A handful of small treats your puppy can easily and quickly eat
2. A quiet, distraction free room
3. The lie down command

Here's how you do it:

Step 1: You should start in a quiet, distraction free room with only you and your puppy. You should put a blanket or carpet on the floor to keep your puppy comfortable. Your puppy will need to start the trick in the lie down position.

With your puppy in the lie down position, kneel down in front of them. Place a treat in front of their face. When your puppy goes for the treat, move it away from them slowly, keeping it close to the ground so your puppy isn't tempted to stand up. Your puppy will follow the treat by crawling across the floor towards it as you move it away. Make sure you move it slowly and not too far at first. After your puppy crawls forward a little bit you can reward them.

Repeat this step a couple of times before moving on. Your puppy should find this trick easier than the others.

Step 2: When your puppy performs the crawl easily and happily then you can move on to adding the verbal command. You can use whatever command you want to. Some favorite commands include "soldier boy, or girl," "army crawl," or just 'crawl.'

Once you have the word command you want to use you can move forward. Repeat step 1 adding the verbal command just before your puppy starts crawling forward. You can do this multiple times to make sure your puppy associates the word with the action.

Step 3: After a while your puppy should be able to associate the verbal command with the action so you can try removing the lure. Show your puppy the treat and use the verbal command. If they do it then you can give them their reward. If they don't then either go back to step 2 or try to mimic the lure action quickly to remind them what you want from them.

This trick is actually a fairly easy one for puppies to do. Don't be surprised if your puppy is able to perform it after only a few tries. It's also okay if your puppy struggles to do it. That means that you just need practice and patience. They'll get the hang of it eventually.

At the end of this trick you want your puppy to crawl along the floor without needing to see a treat or reward, but simply because you told them to using the verbal command.

There are a lot of other tricks you can teach your puppy but these are just the start. Remember that every trick you're going to teach them needs the three basic commands first. If your puppy knows those three commands, they will be able to learn any trick you want to teach them.

If You Enjoyed This Book in Anyway, An Honest Review Is Always Appreciated!

Hey,

Firstly thanks for completing my book this should set you up for success by putting you on the right path.

Remember, there are particular tools that you need not just to make training your dog easier, but make it more effective.

The first crucial tool you will need to make sure you have, so you do not fail, is the dog & puppy training checklist by Bark Insights.

As when starting your pooches training journey, the one thing that anybody who reaches success has; is a detailed checklist to track the progress you have made.

To create a detailed plan to have a mindset shift that you'll need to set you up for success; you have to do endless amounts of research to get mental clarity, acquire new daily habits, and much more.

Creating a checklist yourself is super inconvenient, right?

Well yes, it would be, but luckily for you, I have partnered up with Bark Insights. Who are giving away their highly rated dog & puppy training checklist to help you track your pooches' progress seamlessly!

Best thing about this exclusive offer is it 100% FREE, no-strings-attached. Bark Insights usually charge $49 for this exact same checklist to their customers

All you need to do to claim your FREE the training checklist; is type in on your search browsers URL – free.barkinsights.com

Good luck on your journey and enjoy the checklist!

free.barkinsights.com

www.ingramcontent.com/pod-product-compliance
Ingram Content Group UK Ltd.
Pitfield, Milton Keynes, MK11 3LW, UK
UKHW050711011025
8163UKWH00003B/32